Inside
AMERICAN POLITICS

# Political Action Committees

*By Charlie Samuels*

# LUCENT
PRESS

Published in 2019 by
**Lucent Press, an Imprint of Greenhaven Publishing, LLC**
353 3rd Avenue
Suite 255
New York, NY 10010

For Brown Bear Books Ltd
Editorial Director: Lindsey Lowe
Managing Editor: Tim Cooke
Designer: Lynne Lennon
Design Manager: Keith Davis
Picture Manager: Sophie Mortimer
Children's Publisher: Anne O'Daly

**Picture Credits**
**Front cover:** SAUL LOEB/AFP/Getty Images
**Interior: Alamy:** Prisma by Dukas Presseagentur GmbH/Christian Heeb, 21; **Dreamstime:** Viocera, 9;
**iStock:** alexsi, 5; **Library of Congress:** 11, 12, 14, 16, 17; **Open Access:** AP, 31, Correct the Record, 27,
NBC, 28, Think.progress.org, 39, **Public Domain:** Mark Buckawicki, 19, John Proctor, 18, Michael Vadon,
35, White House/Pete Souza, 23; **Shutterstock:** Katherine Welles, 29, Sergei Brutckii, 38, Orhan Cam, 13,
Diego G Diaz, 43, Drop of Light, 20, Maria Dryfhout, 26, Forest Run, 34, Christopher Halloran, 24,
Karin Hildebrand-Lau, 42, A Katz, 10, 44, lazyllama, 45, Mark Reinstein, 8, Jane Rix, 33, George Sheldon,
4, 7, Joseph Sohm, 6, 25, 32, 37, 40, 41, J Stone, 22, Suzanne Tucker, 36, Tero Vesalainen, 30;
**United States Government:** FEC/Device Daily, 15.

Brown Bear Books has made every attempt to contact the copyright holders.
If you have any information please contact licensing@brownbearbooks.co.uk

**Cataloging-in-Publication Data**

Names: Samuels, Charlie.
Title: Political action committees / Charlie Samuels.
Description: New York : Lucent Press, 2019. | Series: Inside American politics | Includes glossary and index.
Identifiers: ISBN 9781534566651 (pbk.) | ISBN 9781534566668 (library bound) |
ISBN 9781534566675 (ebook)
Subjects: LCSH: Political action committees–United States–Juvenile literature. |
Campaign funds–United States–Juvenile literature.
Classification: LCC JK1991.S26 2019 | DDC 324'.40973–dc23

Printed in the United States of America

CPSIA compliance information: Batch #BW19KL: For further information contact Greenhaven Publishing LLC, New York, New York at 1-844-317-7404.

Please visit our website, www.greenhavenpublishing.com. For a free color catalog of all our
high-quality books, call toll free 1-844-317-7404 or fax 1-844-317-7405.

# Contents

# Chapter 1

# POLITICS
# AND MONEY

Elections in the United States are very expensive. According to one estimate, the 2016 presidential and congressional elections together cost $6.5 billion. Candidates recruit campaign staff, at least some of whom are paid, and hire policy analysts and researchers to help sharpen their message. They have to find premises and pay for transportation, lodgings, and food.

*The primary and general election campaigns that led to the election of Donald Trump as US president in November 2016 are estimated to have cost $2.5 billion.*

Advertising on TV and radio is a major expense. The cost of billboards, **placards**, and campaign literature is also high.

*Few individuals have enough money to fund a federal election campaign.*

The cost of elections means that most candidates, even from the two major political parties, rely on **donations** from private individuals or interest groups to support their campaigns. Some people are concerned that this opens the possibility that donors could have a major influence on the policies of candidates who rely on their money. This might be fine as long as electors are aware of that influence, but what if it is kept hidden? How do electors know who is really bankrolling their candidates?

## Federal Election Campaign Act

US electoral laws work to ensure transparency in campaign finance, particularly to avoid a situation in which wealthy individuals or groups gain too great an influence on local or national politics. The Federal Election Campaign Act (FECA) of 1971 led to the emergence of Political Action Committees (PACs). A PAC is registered when it receives or spends more than $1,000 for the purpose of influencing a federal election. PACs are limited as to how much money they can raise and how they distribute it to candidates.

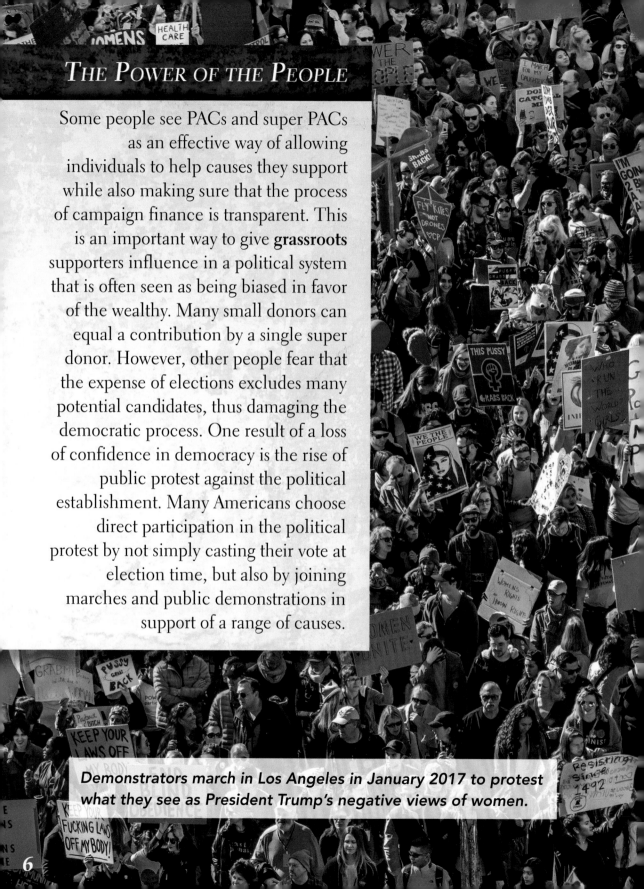

Some people see PACs and super PACs as an effective way of allowing individuals to help causes they support while also making sure that the process of campaign finance is transparent. This is an important way to give **grassroots** supporters influence in a political system that is often seen as being biased in favor of the wealthy. Many small donors can equal a contribution by a single super donor. However, other people fear that the expense of elections excludes many potential candidates, thus damaging the democratic process. One result of a loss of confidence in democracy is the rise of public protest against the political establishment. Many Americans choose direct participation in the political protest by not simply casting their vote at election time, but also by joining marches and public demonstrations in support of a range of causes.

*Demonstrators march in Los Angeles in January 2017 to protest what they see as President Trump's negative views of women.*

## The Super PAC

Amendments to the FECA in 2010 led to the creation of a new type of PAC, known as a super PAC. Super PACs are subject to fewer restrictions than traditional PACs. They can raise and spend unlimited amounts of money. However, they are legally forbidden from financing or even coordinating with the campaigns of specific candidates. In fact, super PACs often get around

*Speaker of the House Paul Ryan raised more than $16 million to help Republican candidates in Congressional elections in 2018.*

these limitations and are able to work closely with campaigns run by the main political parties. Critics feel that PACs and especially super PACs have been created by politicians to ensure that they can continue to get financial support from the wealthiest Americans and corporations. In return, those critics argue, the people who bankroll elections "buy" political influence.

---

### WHAT DO YOU THINK?

The First Amendment gives all Americans free speech. How is it possible to prevent wealthy Americans from having too much influence through political donations without compromising their right to free speech?

# Chapter 2

# WHAT ARE POLITICAL ACTION COMMITTEES?

Elections are potentially momentous events that can affect the whole future of the country. They are frequently won or lost by relatively small margins. That means rival campaigns and candidates are eager to gain any advantage they can. Over time, election laws have tried to regulate these highly competitive situations so that no candidate or party can gain an unfair advantage. In particular, the laws have tried to forbid hidden financial contributions to candidates, whether from corporations, labor unions, or private individuals.

*Spectacular political rallies and conventions cost a lot of money, from booking a venue to setting up media communications.*

The PAC emerged as a response to such laws. PACs are organizations that raise and spend campaign funds to support candidates running for political office. They exist at state level, where they help politicians and **gubernatorial** candidates, but most PACs exist to support candidates who are running in federal elections for the US Congress, as a senator or as a member of the House. PACs also support candidates running for the presidency in primaries or general elections.

*Unions such as the Laborers' International Union can collect voluntary donations from their members to fund PACs.*

## Types of PAC

There are two broad types of PAC. The majority are called connected PACs. They are set up directly by corporations, labor unions, or organizations connected with concerns such as trade or health. They are only allowed to raise money from a specific type of donors, such as managers and shareholders in a business, members of labor unions, or members of a trade board. Unconnected PACs, on the other hand, are completely independent and are free to ask anyone for funds. They are often set up to collect and coordinate support for a particular way of political thinking, such as Christian conservatism or liberal socialism. Unconnected PACs may also promote single issues, such as supporting or opposing gun control or abortion laws.

Another form of PAC is known as a leadership PAC. Leadership PACs are formed by elected officials or national parties to fund a range of other politicians. They are often seen as a way for a politician to use financial influence to gain support within his or her own party. This is usually part of an effort to eventually gain a position of importance, such as becoming a presidential candidate.

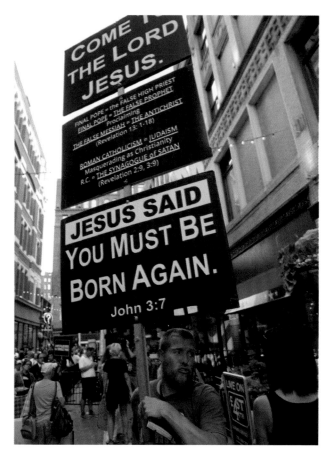

*Christian conservatives have been an influential group in US politics for decades, partly because of their success in raising money to back their preferred candidates.*

## PACs and the Law

Strict laws govern PACs and what they can do. When an organization receives or spends more than $1,000 to influence the result of a federal election, it must register as a PAC with the Federal Election Commission. PACs can raise $5,000 per year from any individual or corporate donor. They can give out $5,000 to a candidate for each campaign, $15,000 to a political party in any year, and $5,000 to another PAC.

## THE POWER OF THE PEOPLE

PACs and super PACs do not only exist at a federal level. They are also used to raise money for gubernatorial campaigns, and for city elections. Supporters of PACs say this enables people to become directly involved in their own government. In 2015, for example, teacher unions and labor unions, such as the United Association of Plumbers and Pipefitters, funded a Louisiana Super PAC called LA Families First. It promoted the Democrat

John Bel Edwards, who won the election for Louisiana governor. Critics of PACs, however, say they also allow billionaires to buy influence in local elections. PACs and super PACs have even supported candidates in elections for school boards.

What gives PACs potentially wide influence, however, is that they can spend unlimited amounts of money on an election independently of funding candidates and parties. A PAC that supports a particular candidate, for example, can finance TV advertising campaigns in his or her favor or—more often—in criticizing his or her opponents.

### WHAT DO YOU THINK?

"Attack ads" are TV commercials that attack the views of a political rival. Why do you think political campaigners believe that they are more effective than ads that promote a positive view?

A PAC is forbidden from coordinating its activities with those of the electoral campaign. In practice, however, PACs are closely in tune with campaigns. They are often run by former staffers of the candidate they support.

## Negative Campaigns

PACs tend to favor attack ads that aim to damage rival candidates. In the 1988 presidential election, for example, the National Security PAC was set up to support Republican candidate George H. W. Bush against the Democratic nominee, Michael Dukakis, governor of Massachusetts. The PAC spent $8.5 million on ads attacking Dukakis. One ad highlighted Dukakis's support for a program that gave prisoners temporary leave. The ad pointed out that, while on leave, a murderer named Willie Horton had committed serious assaults. Such ads severely damaged Dukakis.

*George H. W. Bush waves from a limousine after becoming president in 1989. He defeated Michael Dukakis in the popular votes by 53.4 percent to 45.6 percent.*

*The US Supreme Court decided by a narrow vote that limits on election spending contradicted the constitutional right to free speech of those who wanted to fund political campaigning.*

## Coming of the Super PAC

In 2010, the Supreme Court overturned certain aspects of the FECA, the law that governed campaign finance. That led to the emergence of a new type of PAC, called a super PAC. Unlike other PACs, super PACs cannot give any money directly to candidates or parties. However, there are no limits on the amounts of money a super PAC can raise from individuals or groups, or on how much money they can spend on a particular political campaign.

> **WHAT DO YOU THINK?**
>
> There are no limits on how much money super PACs can raise to support an election campaign. How might this impact elections in the United States?

# Chapter 3

# POLITICAL ACTION COMMITTEES IN HISTORY

Political Action Committees have been around since July 1943, when the first PAC was formed by the Congress of Industrial Organizations (CIO), a federation of labor unions. The CIO collected contributions from its members to campaign for the reelection of President Franklin D. Roosevelt in 1944.

*President Franklin D. Roosevelt (center) benefited from the first PAC for his reelection in 1943.*

The PAC, however, only emerged as an important electoral organization after the passage of the Federal Election Campaign Act (FECA) of 1971, which was revised in 1974. Among other things, the act set out to make the funding of electoral candidates more transparent. At the time, it seemed to some Americans that many candidates were being financially supported by individuals, corporations, and organizations such as labor unions without declaring this support. Voters were concerned this might give candidates' supporters undue influence in Congress or even in the White House.

# The Federal Election Commission

The 1974 FECA limited the amounts that donors could give to individual candidates or national committees, and specified that PACs must disclose their contributors. It also set up the Federal Election Commission (FEC) as a regulatory agency to oversee the implementation of the act. Parties and campaign managers soon realized that PACs could help them get around the limits imposed by the new regulations. By gathering many smaller contributions from a wider range of individuals, they could comply with the law but still raise substantial amounts of money. Four years later, in 1978, the FEC removed limits on donations people could make to political parties, as long as the parties spent it on general politics-related activity rather than on specific candidates or campaigns. This kind of spending became known as soft money. In practice, parties found ingenious ways of using some of it to support their electoral candidates.

*The Federal Election Commission was set up in 1974. It has equal numbers of Republican and Democratic members, so it is often deadlocked over campaign finance reform.*

*President Theodore Roosevelt suggested public funding for presidential campaigns in 1907.*

## Public Funding

Meanwhile, in 1976, the FEC introduced public funding for presidential campaigns. Eligible candidates from recognized political parties could claim up to $20 million to cover their primary and general election campaigns. Parties were also allowed to claim funds to pay for their nominating conventions, although these payments were later withdrawn.

In return for receiving money from the Presidential Election Campaign Fund, which was financed by taxpayer money, candidates had to agree to strict limits on their personal contributions to their own campaigns and not to accept private contributions. Like FECA, public funding was intended to reduce the advantage of wealthy individuals running for the presidency.

Following the FECA, there was a dramatic increase in the number of registered PACs, rising from 600 in the early 1970s to more than 4,000 by 2010. It soon became apparent that, despite the FECA and public funding for presidential campaigns, PACs were actually leading to an increase in the cost of running for office.

## Aggressive Tactics

As PACs became more effective at raising money, they attracted more committed political operatives. In turn, some of these recruits created a more aggressive strategy for raising funds from potential supporters.

There were already concerns about the way in which politicians raised funds for campaigns. For example, in 1972 the reelection campaign of the Republican President Richard M. Nixon had been paid for in part by airline executives. The

*Supporters of Richard Nixon raised money aggressively for his reelection in 1972.*

president's backers effectively threatened that Nixon would refuse to allow the airlines to raise airfares unless their executives made donations to his campaign. The fund-raisers used heavy-handed tactics to gain money from individuals. Some executives tried to claim back their donations from their own company treasuries.

## ┌─ WHAT DO YOU THINK?

Federal funding for presidential campaigns is intended to make it easier for candidates to run in general elections. In what way might it help attract a broader range of candidates?

*Nixon's supporters asked the chairman of American Airlines for a donation equivalent to a quarter of his annual salary.*

Individuals taking money from company funds broke election finance laws. Money for PACs had to be kept separate from a company's main accounts. In all, 18 corporations were found guilty of making illegal contributions to the Nixon campaign. The campaign was successful, however. Nixon easily defeated the Democratic challenger, George McGovern.

## Attempts at Reform

In 1992, the Democrat-controlled Congress passed a bill to restrict the use of soft money. It was **vetoed** by President George H. W. Bush. In 1994, President Bill Clinton proposed a similar bill, but this time it failed to pass through Congress.

## WHAT DO YOU THINK?

Soft money describes funds that are spent not on election campaigns but on broader areas of politics, such as party education and training. How would you ensure that soft money was being used correctly?

# THE POWER OF THE PEOPLE

Local elections are traditionally straightforward. Many people vote for candidates or neighbors they know and trust. Increasingly, however, PACs and super PACs are becoming involved in local campaigns. This can make local elections more confusing. In 2015, for example, a Democratic super PAC named New Jersey Future First spent money to influence a Republican primary election in the township of Parsippany, New Jersey. It later turned out that the super PAC was funded by companies that held contracts with the city government. They were trying to get rid of officials who criticized their city contracts.

*Americans are familiar with posters supporting local candidates. But some people worry that it is becoming more difficult to know what motivates people to fund local campaigns.*

*Senator John McCain (center) and Russ Feingold spent four years bargaining with their congressional colleagues before they finally managed to have their campaign reforms passed into law.*

In 1998, two Congressmen, the Republican John McCain and the Democrat Russ Feingold, sponsored the Bipartisan Campaign Reform Act to amend FECA. After various attempts to pass the bill, it finally became law in 2002. The bill limited the use of soft money and also of **issue-advocacy** ads, which promote particular policies. No broadcast ads were allowed to name a candidate within 60 days of a general election or 30 days of a primary election. Funds from corporations or labor unions could not be used for any ads. McCain later noted, "By the time I became a leading advocate of campaign finance reform, I had come to appreciate that the public's suspicions were not always mistaken. Money does buy access in Washington, and access increases influence that often results in benefiting the few at the expense of the many."

## A Controversial Measure

The Bipartisan Campaign Reform Act, also known as the McCain–Feingold Act, was controversial. Its opponents claimed that it represented an unconstitutional restriction on people's right to free speech, which entitled them to express their political opinions. Soon after the act became law, its legality was challenged in the courts. In 2010, it ended up in the US Supreme Court—where it was overthrown.

*For many Americans, the White House and Washington, D.C., had become dominated by interest groups with access to power.*

## WHAT DO YOU THINK?

A Democrat and a Republican worked together on the Bipartisan Campaign Reform Act. What other issues would benefit from the two main political parties working together instead of opposing each other?

# Chapter 4

# PACS AND
# SUPER PACS TODAY

In *Citizens Utd vs Federal Election Commission* in 2010, the US Supreme Court ruled by five votes to four that the PAC Citizens United had the right to promote a film critical of the Democratic politician Hillary Clinton on TV. The decision effectively overturned the Bipartisan Campaign Reform Act's ban on corporations and unions paying for "electioneering communications."

*Hillary Clinton was the Democratic candidate for president in 2016. She raised more than $800 million through her own committee and her associated super PACs.*

Justice Anthony Kennedy summed up the opinion of the majority of justices: "If the First Amendment has any force, it prohibits Congress from fining or jailing citizens, or associations of citizens, from simply engaging in political speech." On behalf of the minority, Justice John Paul Stevens stated, "A democracy cannot function effectively when

*Barack Obama said of the Supreme Court ruling, "I don't think American elections should be bankrolled by America's most powerful interests."*

its constituent members believe laws are being bought and sold." Among the critics of the ruling was President Barack Obama, who had taken office in 2009. He criticized it in his State of the Union address in 2010.

## Super PACs

The *Citizens Utd* case led to the emergence of super PACs. There was now no limit on how much corporations or individuals could give to a super PAC or how much a super PAC could spend. Despite rules separating super PACs and official campaigns, the two often found informal ways to complement each other. The number of super PACs grew rapidly. In the two years between the court ruling and the 2012 presidential election, super PACs spent $547 million on political advertising.

*Wayne Lapierre of the National Rifle Association (NRA) argues that gun control infringes on the Second Amendment right to bear arms.*

About 76 percent of super PAC spending in the 2012 campaign was spent on negative ads. The NRA, for example, set up the Political Victory Fund. Its ads attacked candidates who supported gun control.

## Anonymous Influence

The main contributors to super PACs were wealthy individuals and for-profit corporations. The organizations did not have to reveal the sources of their money. In many cases the identities of the people or organizations behind a super PAC were hidden behind quite neutral names, such as America Rising. This anonymity led to widespread suspicion of super PACS as a way for the wealthy to buy influence in US politics.

## WHAT DO YOU THINK?

The National Rifle Association opposes any candidate who supports gun control. Some people think the NRA stifles debate on gun control. How might it be justified for an unelected body to have such power?

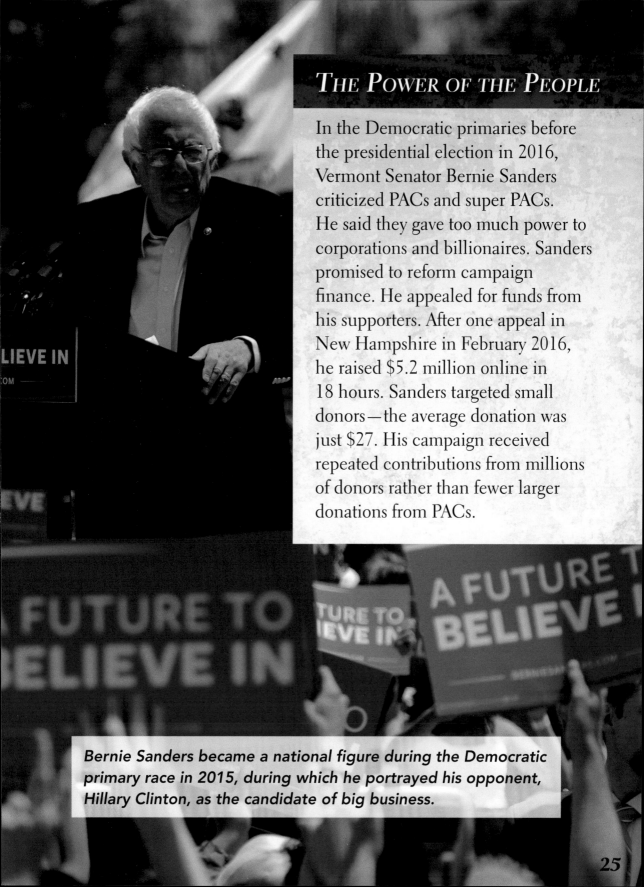

# THE POWER OF THE PEOPLE

In the Democratic primaries before the presidential election in 2016, Vermont Senator Bernie Sanders criticized PACs and super PACs. He said they gave too much power to corporations and billionaires. Sanders promised to reform campaign finance. He appealed for funds from his supporters. After one appeal in New Hampshire in February 2016, he raised $5.2 million online in 18 hours. Sanders targeted small donors—the average donation was just $27. His campaign received repeated contributions from millions of donors rather than fewer larger donations from PACs.

*Bernie Sanders became a national figure during the Democratic primary race in 2015, during which he portrayed his opponent, Hillary Clinton, as the candidate of big business.*

*Republican candidate Mitt Romney raised more than $990 million for the 2012 presidential election campaign.*

In reaction to public suspicion, some politicians began to refuse money from super PACs. They did not want to be seen as being in debt to donors whose identity was not clear. Among those politicians was President Barack Obama, who had already spoken out against super PACs.

However, as Obama began to campaign for reelection in 2012, he found himself at a disadvantage. His Republican opponent, Mitt Romney, was backed by super PACs, and Democrats worried that this gave him an unfair advantage in the campaign. Obama reversed his policy and began to accept the backing of super PACs, too. Obama's campaign manager Jim Messina observed, "We can't allow for two sets of rules in this election." For some people, this was a **hypocritical** move by Obama. For others, it was simply an acknowledgment that the huge amounts of money open to super PACs had helped make elections so expensive that candidates not taking "soft money" were at a great disadvantage.

*PACs such as Correct the Record increasingly divert sizable amounts of revenues to create an online presence for candidates by sponsoring websites and social media sites.*

## The 2016 Election and Primaries

The 2016 election was fought between Hillary Clinton for the Democrats and Donald J. Trump for the Republicans. Clinton was a former first lady and Secretary of State. She was supported by many wealthy donors. Compared with Trump, she appeared as the candidate of "big money." A Clinton super PAC, named Hillary for America, raised $563.8 million. Her challenger in the Democratic primaries, Senator Bernie Sanders, attracted many votes from Clinton, partly by arguing that it was not right that billionaires could buy elections. Donald Trump, on the

**WHAT DO YOU THINK?**

Although he opposed super PACs, Barack Obama ended up being supported by them. What justification might he have had for having changed his mind?

other hand, was seen as a **maverick** whose policies put him at odds with the Republican Party. In the primaries, he faced party heavyweights such as Mario Rubio, Ted Cruz, and Jeb Bush. Bush's father and brother had both been US presidents. Jeb Bush had been governor of Florida for eight years. He was backed by a super PAC named Right to Rise, which raised more than $115 million. Despite this financial advantage, however, he lost the nomination to Trump. One explanation is that, while Bush's campaign targeted Trump, Right to Rise targeted Marco Rubio, who was expected to be Bush's main rival.

Trump went on to win the presidential election in December 2016. He won the majority of votes in the electoral college, although not in the popular vote. Trump's

*Jeb Bush was the favorite to be the Republican candidate, but lost to Donald Trump.*

## WHAT DO YOU THINK?

In the 2016 election campaign, Donald Trump gained TV exposure largely by saying controversial things, rather than by paying for ads. In what ways might this have influenced the kinds of policies he announced?

*Trump's campaign attracted attention by maintaining a high profile in the news media, as well as through advertising.*

success startled election observers. He had been backed by his own super PACs, but the sums they raised were far smaller than those raised to support Bush's primary campaign or Clinton's election campaign.

Trump's campaign turned ideas about elections and election funding on their head. Even without PACs and super PACs bankrolling ads on his behalf, Trump dominated the election news on TV. His unconventional approach earned him so much free exposure on news shows that he needed less support from paid-for TV advertisements. He asserted that Mexicans were criminals and that he would build a wall along the border. He claimed that Hillary Clinton should be locked up for treason and promised to "drain the swamp" in Washington, D.C. Such announcements made sure that his media exposure remained higher than that of his rivals.

The defeat of Jeb Bush in the primaries and Hillary Clinton in the presidential election had shown that even the backing of millions of dollars via PACs and super PACs could not guarantee electoral success. It was not clear, however, whether this was a general rule or whether it simply reflected the desire of the public at the time to elect an outsider who would shake up US politics.

## A Constant Campaign

As soon as he took office in January 2017, Trump announced the start of his campaign for reelection in 2020. Within a year, PACs and super PACs supporting the president had spent more than $1 million on ads supporting his policies and criticizing his rivals—both within and outside the Republican Party.

*As a candidate, and also as president, Donald Trump used Twitter to communicate his thoughts directly to his supporters, decreasing his reliance on advertising to promote his ideas.*

Meanwhile, the mainstream Republican Mitch McConnell, the Senate Majority Leader, was aligned with a super PAC called the Senate Leadership Fund. Its goal was to increase the Republican majority in the Senate. In 2016, it spent most of its total of $114 million opposing Democratic candidates.

*Steve Bannon (left) raised money for a campaign to promote what he termed "nationalist" Republicans.*

In 2018, the Senate Leadership Fund also targeted Republican candidates supported by President Trump's former advisor Steve Bannon. Bannon had vowed to unseat mainstream Republicans and replace them with more **extremist** candidates. McConnell's super PAC was supported by another PAC called One Nation and a married couple from Las Vegas, the billionaire Sheldon Adelson and his wife, Miriam, who together gave $35 million.

## WHAT DO YOU THINK?

PACs and super PACs support rival Republican politicians with very different views of the party's future. Is that good for party democracy, or does it suggest that the party will eventually damage itself?

# Chapter 5

# CONTROVERSIES
# AND DEBATES

One of Donald Trump's most popular slogans during his election campaign in 2016 was "Drain the swamp." It appealed to **disillusioned** voters who thought politics was a corrupt process in which politicians, **lobbyists**, civil servants, and others operated for their own advantage. For these voters, campaign finance is another area in which politics does not work for the good of the American people. Some observers suggest that PACs and super PACs have made things worse.

Because donors can hide behind anonymity, it seems as if the action committees are a way for the wealthy to buy influence. The lack of transparency makes the organizations appear suspicious, even when they are not.

*Many Americans were attracted by Donald Trump's verbal tirades describing Washington, D.C., as a swamp of corruption.*

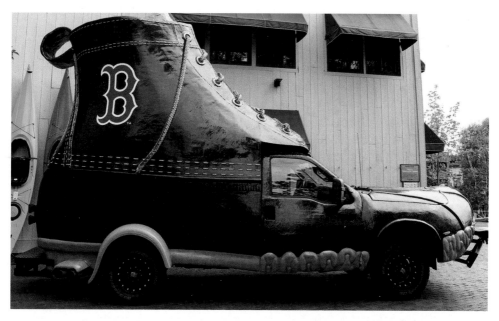

*In 2017, Linda Bean, of the retailer L.L. Bean, was found guilty of giving too much money to a PAC supporting Donald Trump.*

## Wealthy Individuals

The PAC system is increasingly accused of giving too much power to wealthy individuals. In 2016 and 2017, for example, the Republican businessman Richard Uihlein gave $15 million to PACs and super PACs. More than $4 million went to PACs supporting the US Senate campaign of Wisconsin politician Kevin Nicholas. Democrats said Uihlein was "buying" the seat.

According to research, donors have little influence over politicians after their election. However, former Congressman Barney Frank observed, "Elected officials are the only human beings in the world who are supposed to take large sums of money on a regular basis from absolute strangers without it having any effect on their behavior."

## Rising Costs

PACs and super PACs have made elections more expensive. The 2016 federal election campaign was the most expensive in history. As soon as one side increases its spending on TV and radio slots, and social media platforms, everyone else buys more exposure, too, pushing costs higher and higher. It may therefore become more difficult for candidates not backed by PACs and super PACs to have a fair chance in an election campaign.

In the same way, critics feel that PACs and super PACs make political debate more extreme. Groups that stick to single issues, such as gun control or the right to life, tend to take a black-and-white view. More general PACs and super PACs also often emphasize extremes rather than

graduated views. Political staffers sometimes complain that activists involved with PACs and super PACs are too idealistic for the **pragmatic** world of politics.

*Radio slots are less expensive than TV ads, but they are also seen as being less effective in influencing voters.*

## Open to Abuse

PACs and super PACs can be open to abuse. "Scam PACs" raise money for political uses, but spend most of it on administrative charges. In 2013 to 2015, for example, a Republican PAC called the Tea Party Leadership Fund raised $6.7 million, mainly from Republicans angry about the policies of Barack Obama. However, about 87 percent of the money was spent on running costs. Only $910,000 went to support candidates. In Texas in 2012, the candidate Allen West asked the FEC to stop PACs raising money in his name because they were making no contribution to supporting his campaign.

*Allen West tried to stop PACs raising money in his name, but the FEC later ruled the PACs had not broken any rules.*

## WHAT DO YOU THINK?

Allen West believed that scam PACs were using his campaign to raise money, but not then giving the money to him. How could such a practice be prevented in the future?

# THE POWER OF THE PEOPLE

In 2010, the Republican politician Scott Walker was elected governor of Wisconsin. In 2012, citizens concerned with his policies limiting the rights of state employees forced a recall election. Walker raised more than $30 million to support his campaign. Much of the money came from outside Wisconsin. His opponent, the Democrat Tom Barrett, raised $4 million, mainly within Wisconsin. Walker defeated Barrett with an increased majority. He was later put on trial for coordinating his campaign with the activities of a super PAC named Wisconsin Club for Growth. In 2015, the Wisconsin Supreme Court cleared him. Walker ran in the Republican presidential primaries in 2015, but dropped out early.

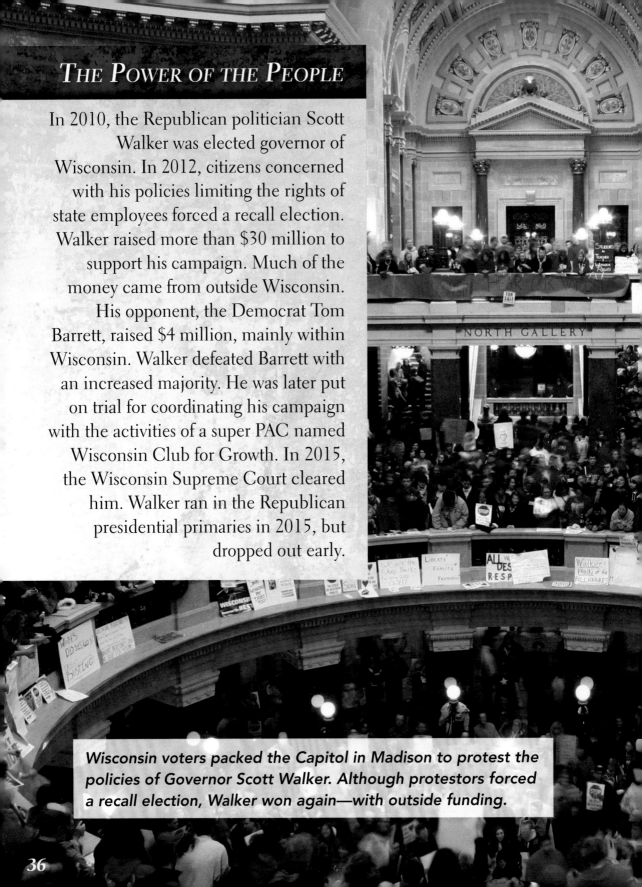

*Wisconsin voters packed the Capitol in Madison to protest the policies of Governor Scott Walker. Although protestors forced a recall election, Walker won again—with outside funding.*

*Some people believe that the whole cost of politics in the United States is too expensive. They say that the government has no right to spend money that belongs to the citizens.*

## Money for Nothing?

Perhaps the most damaging criticism of PACs and super PACs is that they do not work. In 2016, Donald Trump defeated Jeb Bush in the Republican primaries and Hillary Clinton in the presidential election, even though both were backed by far more money than him. In the 2012 election, American Crossroads, a Republican super PAC, spent more than $100 million to try to ensure that Barack Obama would not be elected for a second term. Not only was Obama reelected, but only three of the twenty federal candidates backed by American Crossroads won their races. The huge expenditure had achieved virtually no gain.

### ━ WHAT DO YOU THINK? ━

Some donors gave millions of dollars to American Crossroads to fight Barack Obama and his policies. How might they have reacted when Republican candidates did so badly in the 2012 election?

# Chapter 6

# PACS, SUPER PACS, AND YOU

PACs and super PACs are at the heart of political life, particularly during election campaigns. During these times, the TV, radio, and newspapers seem to be full of election-related advertisements. Billboards line highways. Some have a message about general issues, while others attack particular candidates for various weaknesses. Much of this material is paid for by PACs and super PACs.

*One famous attack ad in 1964 showed a girl playing with daisies before a nuclear bomb detonated.*

In 2010, Democrats in Congress proposed a law that the people who run PACs and super PACs would have to appear in their own ads, in the same way that candidates have to endorse their own ads. However, the legislation failed to pass. That leaves American citizens in a situation where they do not know precisely who is sending them election messages. In 2017, for example, a PAC named Josh Mandel for US Senate supported a campaign in Ohio.

Mandel was a Republican campaigning for a seat in the US Senate. Unknown to many voters, however, a large number of the backers of the PAC came from outside the state, so their interests in Ohio were not clear.

## Approaches for Money

It is possible that you might be approached by activists raising funds for PACs or super PACs. Making financial contributions to support causes is one way many individual Americans play an increased role in politics, rather than simply joining a party or voting in elections. However, the rise of what are called "scam PACs" has led to a situation in which some fund-raisers exploit people's political frustrations to raise money, without spending it responsibly.

**PACs such as Restore Our Future, which supported Republican Mitt Romney in the presidential election in 2012, use urgent appeals to try to raise funds from donors.**

*Bringing together platforms of star speakers such as these civil rights activists requires funding to pay for travel costs.*

Often, fund-raisers use urgent appeals. A message from a PAC linked with the Tea Party movement said, "Your immediate contribution could be the most important financial investment you will make to return America to greatness." Rather than react to such sales pitches, take time to research organizations to find out which spends most of its funds on campaigning. Unlike businesses, PACs and super PACs have no legal obligation to spend their funds in a particular way. They are not audited, they are not controlled by directors, and they have no specific responsibility to their donors.

## WHAT DO YOU THINK?

Fund-raisers sometimes use aggressive marketing techniques to gain money for political causes. In what ways might politics be considered different from other areas of marketing?

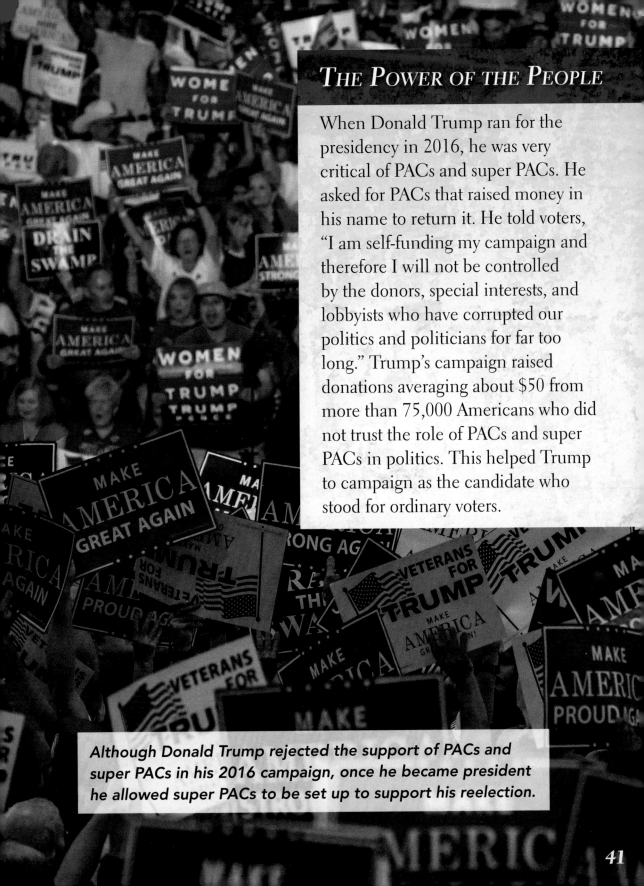

## THE POWER OF THE PEOPLE

When Donald Trump ran for the presidency in 2016, he was very critical of PACs and super PACs. He asked for PACs that raised money in his name to return it. He told voters, "I am self-funding my campaign and therefore I will not be controlled by the donors, special interests, and lobbyists who have corrupted our politics and politicians for far too long." Trump's campaign raised donations averaging about $50 from more than 75,000 Americans who did not trust the role of PACs and super PACs in politics. This helped Trump to campaign as the candidate who stood for ordinary voters.

*Although Donald Trump rejected the support of PACs and super PACs in his 2016 campaign, once he became president he allowed super PACs to be set up to support his reelection.*

41

# GETTING
# INVOLVED

**P**eople have contrasting views of the role of PACs and super PACs in the political system. For their supporters, they allow individuals to become directly involved in supporting political causes in which they believe. For their critics, they are more a way of giving political influence to wealthy individuals and corporations. If you believe strongly in a cause, donating to a PAC may be something you would find rewarding. However, before doing so it is worth checking the group's activities. How much money does it raise overall? How much of what it raises is actually spent on political campaigning, rather than administration?

*If you believe strongly in particular policies, it is possible to join and volunteer for a political party in your area.*

## THE POWER OF THE PEOPLE

On some occasions, Americans prefer to make their opinions known in a more direct way than by contributing funds to election campaigns. In 2018, campaigns to increase gun control and to support the rights of the children of illegal immigrants, called Dreamers, brought millions of Americans on to the streets. They carried banners and shouted slogans. Organizers know that if protests are large enough, they will gain TV exposure for their cause without having to pay for expensive ads.

A Latina wears a T-shirt proclaiming her status as a "Dreamer" during a 2017 rally against President Trump's reluctance to renew legislation protecting her and other young people.

*One way of making your voice heard is to join in a protest—and shout!*

## Pay Your Way

If you do not think PACs and super PACs are for you, it is still possible to support the causes in which you believe. You can donate money directly to a candidate's campaign, for example. The maximum donation is $2,700 per candidate per election. People under 18 years old can donate to politicians, as long as they use their own money and they are aware that the donation is being made. These measures are intended to prevent adults from making illegal donations under children's names.

If you want to be more directly involved, politicians always need help during election campaigns. Volunteers stuff envelopes for mail-outs, knock on doors to raise support, distribute publicity material, and call potential voters.

## WHAT DO YOU THINK?

Young Americans can donate money to political campaigns before they are old enough to vote, at age 18. How might you ensure that young people who are interested in politics can make their voices heard?

You could contact the campaign headquarters and volunteer to help. Campaigning can be demanding work, however—only undertake it if you are fully committed to the cause. The same is true if you decide to volunteer to work directly for a PAC or super PAC, perhaps calling voters to try to raise money. Make sure the organization is a good fit for your views before giving it your time for free.

## Your Vote Matters

The rise of PACs and super PACs does not mean that there is no role for individuals in the election process. No matter how much money someone pays toward a campaign, everyone is equally entitled to express their opinions. All citizens are entitled to just one vote—and all votes have the same value, no matter who casts them.

*Some people see elections as a chance to remind politicians that they work for the good of the American people.*

# Glossary

**disillusioned:** disappointed that something is not as good as had been expected

**donations:** sums of money given to organizations such as charities

**extremist:** someone who holds extreme political or religious views

**grassroots:** involving ordinary people as the basis of an organization

**gubernatorial:** related to a governorship or a governor

**hypocritical:** pretending that one has higher values or standards than one does

**issue-advocacy:** advertising related to broad political ideas rather than specific campaigns or candidates

**lobbyists:** people who attempt to influence political or other leaders to create or change particular legislation

**maverick:** unorthodox or independently minded

**placards:** printed or handwritten signs for public display

**pragmatic:** dealing with things in a sensible and practical way, rather than an ideological way

**vetoed:** used presidential power to refuse to authorize a new law

# For More Information

## Books

**Cunningham, Kevin.** *How Political Campaigns and Elections Work.* How the US Government Works. Minneapolis, MN: Core Library, 2015.

**Donovan, Sandy.** *Special Interests: From Lobbyists to Campaign Funding.* Inside Elections. Minneapolis, MN: Lerner Publications, 2015.

**Peterchuck, David.** *PACs, Super PACS, and Fundraising.* American Politics Today. St Louis, MO: Turtleback Books, 2016.

## Websites

**What Are PACs?**
*https://www.opensecrets.org/pacs/pacfaq.php*
A description of PACs, with links to lists of all current PACs and super PACs.

**What Is a Super PAC?**
*https://www.thoughtco.com/what-is-a-super-pac-3367928*
A article describing the influence of super PACs and how they operate.

# Index